# LEADERSHIP SKILLS FOR MANAGERS SIMPLIFIED

## MASTER THE BASICS OF BECOMING A GOOD BOSS

### GREG L. ALSTON

ALCHEMY PUBLISHING GROUP

Alchemy Publishing Group Savannah, Georgia

www.alchemy-publishing.com

ISBNS:

Ebook Kindle.    978-1-63297-002-2

Paperback.      978-1-63297-023-7

Hardback.       978-1-63297-024-4

Originally published as the Ten Things a New manager Must Get Right From The Start in 2014. The book has been significantly revised and updated with fresh content for this printing

Published in the United States of America

# CONTENTS

# FREE GIFT FOR MY READERS

Portions of this book were originally published in 2014 as the Ten Things a New Manager Must Get Right from the Start. Based on feedback from hundreds of readers, I have made significant improvements to this book from the previous version. The book received excellent reviews from many readers, but some left bad reviews based upon the inclusion of material from my book, *The Bosshole Effect*.

My aim was to provide a helpful outline for new managers to become great bosses. I thought including material from my more detailed book would be helpful. But some people did not perceive it that way. I apologize for the misunderstanding and have changed the new edition to avoid this conflict of interest. The new edition now has a more focused approach on learning how to manage people at work, as I have added new material and updated much of the narrative. Hopefully, you will enjoy this updated post-Pandemic version of the book.

As always, you, the reader, are in control and I appreciate your honest feedback. Without your support, I would have no audience. Let me know your opinion on the new edition once you've read it.

Management and leadership are not well-taught in our educational system. I designed this book for employees who are concerned they may not be ready to assume a leadership position. If you do not feel fully prepared to show up on Monday morning with the confidence that you can be a great boss, then this book is for you.

Once you are the boss, your colleagues see you differently. Your former acquaintances will now be your subordinates. They will observe you to make sure the new job has not gone to your head. They will be skeptical until you earn their trust.

New managers often struggle with the transition to becoming a boss. As a result, they alienate people and damage their ability to lead. This management and leadership primer will set you on the right track. Build a productive team by executing the effective strategies I have included in this book.

Wishing you luck on your team-building journey. The aim is to become a skilled manager by leading, not bossing, people around. No-one likes a bossy boss. People join excellent companies but quit bad bosses. The work environment post COVID is different. Employees are much less willing to put up with stupid rules. They are much more likely to "quit quietly" and ignore orders they don't like. As a result, it has never been more important to keep your employees engaged and enthusiastic about delivering great service to your customers. I hope you find this book useful.

As a special Thank You to my loyal readers, I am offering you this gift just for looking at my book. In Chapter 8 and Chapter 9, I explain **The Amazing One Page Employee Manual and the 24 trait employee rating system that drives it.** I use these tools to get the best out of my teams. Even if you don't buy this book, please accept this gift as a thank you for checking it out.

# INTRODUCTION

**Leadership Skills for Managers Simplified**

Leadership is a lost art. Good leadership requires commitment, ethics, and morals. Poor leadership simply requires funding. It's not surprising that so few people become good leaders when morality is under attack and evil is glorified.

People are so entrenched in their political views that nobody engages in dialogue. And it is not helping our nation thrive. Too many groups seek to divide us into camps and put us at war with each other. And the time for this to stop is now.

One person can't change the world. But you can make a difference for the people you work with by becoming a leader who uses critical thinking skills, emotional intelligence, and compassion for others to unite people in the common purpose of creating a successful business. When we pull together to achieve a common goal, we overlook our superficial differences to become a team. Good teams are made of people willing to pull together to accomplish goals. Race, color, creed, religion, gender, pronouns, national origin, and political persuasions should not be a barrier to becoming a valuable member of the team. And outstanding leaders are skilled at uniting people around a common goal.

Through working together, we can unite and make good stuff happen and tell those who seek to divide us to pound sand. If we don't refocus our work on providing value to our customers, the business will fail.

Life is not that complicated. Academics and elites of all persuasions make it appear convoluted. My aim with this book is to provide you with a simple framework for improving your leadership skills. When you become a better leader, good things will happen.

**Why is this Important?**

There are many forces at work in our country actively trying to divide us into camps and pit us against each other. The loudest voices are not always the wisest voices. I choose to believe that each of us has much more in common with our neighbors than popular opinion seems to trumpet. Regardless of the race, color, gender, age, religion or any other subset of humans to which we belong I think there are only two kinds of people in the world.

The first kind of person is a good person. Good people wake up every day trying to do good things. Sometimes good people do bad things but they feel bad about it. In general good people go about their day trying to do what's right, trying to manage their lives as best as possible, and trying to make a good life for themselves and their family. The vast majority of people in America are good people.

The second kind of person is an evil person. This person wakes up every day, trying to cheat, rob, injure, and damage other people. They do this because they like to do it. They don't care about how their actions affect their neighbors. They simply want what they want, and they're going to take it. Sometimes these evil people do good things but it's purely by accident. Most of the time, they are looking to get away with something by taking advantage of someone else.

Rather than create artificial or superficial reasons to hire someone, the use of the correct character traits and behavioral anchors will allow you to focus on identifying whether your employee or potential employee is a good person or an evil person. If the person is continually trying to do the right thing, but needs some help to get better, they are likely a good person and worth your time and effort.

If the person is dishonest, deceitful, addicted, damaged, or unable to meet the behavioral needs of the job, then they are not worth your time and effort. Notice that nothing in these descriptive terms deals with their gender, their race, or their surface identity in any way. By focusing on the behaviors required to do your job, you will automatically create a hiring system that is fair and inclusive. The system will be based on what people can do not what they look like. And after all, isn't that the goal of fair employment practices?

I firmly believe in Martin Luther King Jr.'s dream that we should all be judged by the content of our character and not the color of our skin. Character is colorblind, religion blind, gender blind, and identity blind. Lawyers and bureaucrats go out of their way to make life more complicated than it needs to be. I prefer to look at it in the opposite way. Make life as simple as it can be.

Hire good people and teach them how to do their jobs. If one of your employees is an evil person, then get them out of your company as quickly as possible. Base your decisions on objective behavioral anchors and your assessment will be as accurate as it can be. The only criteria that matters in your hiring process is, is this person able to do the job for which I am hiring them and do it well.

Don't get caught up in any of the politically charged nonsense being bantered about. Entering that debate serves no real purpose. As a business person, manager, leader, your job is to identify, hire, train and lead people who can help you accomplish the vision and mission of your organization. If you select them based on the character traits above the accuracy of your hiring will dramatically improve.

**What this book is not**

This book is not a comprehensive step-by-step guide to everything you have to do to be an influential leader. It is, however, an easy-to-read primer to help you develop the leadership skills you need to thrive. Reading this book will not make you a good leader, but it will help you understand what you need to do better. I have been doing this for 45 plus years and there is no way to put all that I have learned into one book. It would be too long and it would be difficult to use.

This book is the appetizer, my website leadershipraptor.com will be the main course. I hope you enjoy the journey. Please let me know if you need anything.

**I'm a Manager, Now What?**

Every day, someone becomes a new manager of a department, unit, business, or organization. Regardless of the level of experience you have in your previous job, nothing truly prepares you to take on an entirely new job in management. Management differs from non-management work. You are now responsible for others' work. Others will look to you for guidance and support, decisions and policy. There is nothing more exhilarating than getting your first promotion. Nothing is scarier than managing people. People come in a variety of sizes, shapes, and with different motivations. It is hard to teach a group to work together. Your success as a manager depends on your ability to lead a team to produce quality work.

So while you're excited about a promotion, there could be a nagging feeling that you may not be ready. Starting a new job or role always involves uncertainty, regardless of personal confidence. With my experience, I can make your transition more successful and simple.

I want to show my knowledge by recounting a story of my transition to a new management job. My 10+ years of management experience allowed me to deal with this event satisfactorily. Imagine being a new manager faced with this scenario.

In 1990, the Vice President of Pharmacy hired me at Thrifty Drug Stores in Southern California to take over as the pharmacy manager of the Beverly Hills location. This location was one of the top five stores in the chain for prescription volume but was being poorly managed. The vice president and I had worked together at a previous company, so he trusted me to take over this high-volume location. I had not yet received training on Thrifty Drug's prescription dispensing software and systems because I was new to the company. The pharmacy team uses the prescription dispensing software for various tasks. These include inputting prescriptions, printing labels, filling prescriptions and counseling patients.

No two pharmacy systems are identical and they use different terminology and short codes to operate. Before the store opened on Monday, I was supposed to meet the old manager for orientation before opening the store. I arrived 45 minutes early, got the key from the store manager, and entered the pharmacy to familiarize myself with the surroundings. The store was going to open at 9 o'clock.

At 8:45, the first pharmacy technician showed up to work, but no pharmacist appeared. Since customers were gathering in front of the pharmacy, I opened it at 9 o'clock, when I was the only pharmacist in the building. Monday mornings are the most hectic times in a community pharmacy. And this Monday was no exception. 40 to 50 customers were in line, waiting to fill prescriptions. Unfortunately, the pharmacist didn't come to orient me to the software as planned. I did not how to switch on the pharmacy computers. I know this is difficult for you to understand in the modern age, but the computer was a huge 4 x 4 foot box housed in the building's basement. Computer knowledge was not as prevalent because home computers were not yet being in widespread use. Within 15 minutes, I powered up the computers, but was still unsure about how to operate the software. The customers grew in number and became unruly.

The summary of my first day managing a drugstore in Beverly Hills:

- I received no training in the systems.

- I was unfamiliar with my colleagues.

- The phones were ringing off the hook and the computer systems were down.

- The staff was not well trained and not focused on customer service.

- Customers in the waiting area were ready to fight.

Four clerks and two technicians were awaiting my guidance to help them do their jobs and keep them from getting yelled at.

They waited to see my next move. The team was not functioning well. Their goal was to do the minimum to stay employed. I could feel them watching me to see what I would do.

My initial emotional reaction was to lock the door and leave. No one could operate effectively as a manager under those conditions right? However, I used my professional experience to navigate the day successfully. I could therefore earn respect from those employees and customers.

I want to ask you a simple question before revealing what I did. What would you have done? You can see what I did at the end of Chapter Six. If you can resolve this situation and develop your team, you don't need this book. If you are less certain that you would've been able to handle the situation; I suggest you continue reading.

Admitting not knowing everything is crucial for new managers to succeed. Having the title "manager" doesn't mean you know more than anyone else. It simply means you must get the work done.

Step two involves seeking advice from those with experience. You shouldn't expect to handle complex issues without receiving specific training. In the real world, training happens on-the-job, not in a classroom. While in school you listen to the lecture, then you take the test. Problems happen in real time in the real world. So, unlike in academia, you can face the test before you get the training.

The book doesn't aim to teach all aspects of management. Becoming a competent boss will take years and multiple experiences. You can get there faster if you learn the secrets I am sharing with you in this book.

This book is intentionally short. As a college professor, I found I was much more successful at helping students learn a skill when I focused on one problem and one solution at a time. Being transparent about the goal and staying concise helps to pinpoint errors, devise solutions, and reach success. A 300-page book would be overwhelming and unusable for quickly preparing you to be a good leader and manager.

**So here's what I suggest you do.**

- Carve out some quiet time to read this book through in its entirety. The chapters will guide you through the skills you need to become an excellent manager.

- While you are reading this book, keep a notepad and pencil by your side. Jot down the chapter, page, and reason when it resonates with your situation.

- Note down the top three changes you need to make to become a successful new manager after reading the chapter.

- Use the book as a resource for work concerns.

- Let me know your issue, and I'll try to guide you.

There is an iconic scene in the movie, The Iron Lady starring Meryl Streep as Margaret Thatcher when she is being interviewed by a physician in the hospital. The doctor is trying to determine whether she has slipped into a state of dementia. He asks her, "How are you feeling?" Mrs. Thatcher responds by chastising the doctor for caring more about feelings than thoughts and ideas. She then launches into a monologue that I believe is well worth repeating. If you prefer to see the YouTube video, you can watch this movie clip at the following link:

"Watch your thoughts because they become your words. Watch your words because they become your actions. Watch your actions because they become your habits. Watch your habits because they become your character. And watch your character because it becomes your destiny. What we think is what we become."

These powerful words describe the logic behind a successful "leadership" mindset. Understanding how your thoughts and actions affect your team's performance is crucial to your new management role. Thoughts shape actions. The way you act will influence how your employees act. The behavior you model will become the expectation for your team. With that in mind, this short book helps you understand the essentials of managing employees. Remember that your employees are watching everything you do. Saying one thing and doing another kills employee engagement. If you fail them, they will look for another job and you will lose the enormous investment your company has made in their training and development. The book will concentrate on core themes critical to good management and leadership.

As you read this book, I would ask you to do me two favors. If I can provide more clarity about a manager's role let me know. My primary concern in writing this book is that the information I am providing to you is useful. Without your feedback, I will never know. So please go to the following page on my blog and leave a comment for me. I will read them and respond to the best of my ability. https://www.leadershipraptor.com/Question

Second, I would ask that after you read this book, please go on to Amazon.com. Login to the account you used to buy the book and write a brief review providing your honest opinion of the quality and usefulness of the book? Your review will help me see if I conveyed the message correctly. There are a ton of inferior quality books being written and published these days by ghost writers. I want to assure you I am a real person with actual experiences. I have done everything I talk about and I genuinely have your interest at heart. I want to make sure that I am helping you succeed. Please write a review for the book on Amazon.

# Chapter 1: The Three Things Employees Want From You

**The COVID Pandemic Rocked our World**

Businesses had to close, and they paid workers to stay home or shifted to remote work. Over 6 million people left the workforce because of the pandemic, which completely upended the way things used to be. Many job openings didn't receive any applicants. It was a strange time and a strange world. Other than that, everything was just fine. But the dynamics of the workplace changed.

The Gallup organization released the State of the Global Workforce1 report in May 2023. This report developed some interesting findings.

The percentage of employees thriving at work reached a record high of 23 percent in the year 2022. The good news is a record high, the bad news is that only 23 percent of workers feel engaged at work. Engaged employees find their work meaningful and feel connected to their organization. They take ownership of their performance and they support their teammates. Unfortunately, this means that 77% percent of employees are not engaged. They fall into one of two categories.

The first category is called **Quiet Quitting** and 59% of employees are in this group. These employees are simply taking up space and watching the clock. Their goal is to do the minimum to keep from getting fired. Although they are barely productive, they are more likely to be stressed and burned out. They feel lost and disconnected from their workspace.

The remaining 18% of employees are **Loud Quitting**. These employees undermine the organization, undercuts its goals and oppose their leaders. They do not trust their employer.

Gallup estimates that low engagement costs the global economy 8.8 Trillion dollars per year. The human toll on stress, burnout and loss of joy is staggering. Forty-four percent of employees reported experiencing a lot of stress at work the previous day. Globally, over 51% of currently employed workers reported they are looking for or actively seeking a new job.

Why does any of this matter? Because a business needs engaged customers who promote. the business to their friends and family. Companies with engaged customers are much more profitable. Engaged employees create engaged customers when they enthusiastically serve them. A **Quitting** employee irritates customers and prevents them from becoming engaged.

Let me explain this differently. Suppose you owned a soccer team that had ten players on the field. Given the statistics I just shared, this means that two of your players are actively trying to help the team win the game. Six members of your team don't care if the team wins or loses. And two members of your team are actively trying to score goals for the other team. How can you possibly achieve greatness within that team dynamic?

Employees decide and take actions every day that affect your organization. How you treat employees affects your organization's success..

Employee engagement research shows higher profits when employees are engaged. Gallup analyzed the differences between the top 25% of business and the bottom 25% of businesses. The results are overwhelming.

The top quartile of businesses experienced:

- 81% less absenteeism

- 58% less safety accidents

- 18% less turnover for high turnover companies

- 43% less turnover for low turnover companies

- 28% less shrinkage (theft from the company)

- 10% increase in customer loyalty

- 18% increase in sales

- 23% increase in profitability

And the most important finding of all is that 70% of the variance in team engagement is determined solely by the manager. Employee engagement should be a manager's primary role responsibility.

Managers inform employees on their duties, back them up, and show how their work supports success. To succeed in that responsibility, managers need to learn when to coach, when to take command and when to create a positive environment. Managers don't talk meaningfully, so the employees view them as micromanaging.

Leaders must:

1. Redefine managers' roles and expectations as defined in this book.

2. Provide the resources and development that managers need to coach and meet those expectations.

3. Create employee evaluation systems that help managers accurately assess performance, hold employees accountable, and coach excellence.

Gallup has created the Q12 survey to identify the 12 needs managers can meet to improve employees' productivity. These 12 needs make up their engagement survey. Here are the twelve questions included:

1. I know what they expect of me at work.

2. I have the materials and equipment I need to do my work right.

3. At work, I can do what I do best every day.

4. In the last seven days, I have received recognition or praise for doing good work.

5. My supervisor, or someone at work, seems to care about me as a person.

6. There is someone at work who encourages my development.

7. At work, my opinions seem to count.

8. The mission or purpose of my company makes me feel my job is important.

9. My fellow employees are committed to doing quality work.

10. I have a best friend at work.

11. In the last six months, someone at work has talked to me about my progress.

12. This last year, I have had opportunities at work to learn and grow.

**Your Mindset as a Manager**

A manager's mindset affects the team's performance. Too many new managers think their job is to tell employees what to do. This bias against employees is a problem.

During the industrial revolution, few employees were literate. Bosses designed the factory management structure to manage illiterate workers. Managers told the employees what to do. They were smart and managed the business. The workers made products. They didn't need to be smart.

The world has changed. However, many people's view of management have not changed. Management practices founded in the industrial production are not suitable for our service-based economy. Workers are more educated, more experienced, and less likely to accept dictatorial management styles.

Treating your employees as less smart will put you in a difficult position. A manager who claims to have all the answers harms their leadership ability. With a more collaborative leadership style, your team will thrive. Your mindset will determine not only your self-talk but the way you speak out loud to your employees. The words you use when you talk to your employees will determine the response that you get from them. Regardless of your intention, if you use the wrong words, you will be unsuccessful at becoming a good boss.

Thoughts become your words. Words become your actions. Actions become your habits. Habits become your leadership style. Your leadership style will determine the character of your leadership. And your character of your leadership will determine your success as a leader.

What mindset do you need for management success? Simply put, you must have a leadership rather than management mindset. Supervisors "manage" things and processes, but bosses "lead" people. If you manage people, you will fail at leadership. I'll share two short stories about my former bosses to explain what I mean.

The first fellow I will describe is a person who we will call Dick. Dick became the Vice President of pharmacy when I was a regional pharmacy manager for the company. All six regional pharmacy managers had an average of 15 years of experience in middle management. None of us had ever met Dick before he appeared at our executive meeting at the headquarters building. I've met no one as unpleasant as him. Within 15 minutes of his introduction, he had accused every one of us of being stupid and incompetent. He had insulted each of us based on our personal appearance, heritage, and ancestry or work history. He told us he'd fire us if we didn't follow his orders. Following the meeting, I began seeking alternative employment. No one wants to be treated with that level of disrespect. It took me almost six months to escape that hellhole. In the meantime, I did not behave as a model employee. The clown sucked the job dry of its energy and enthusiasm.

The second person I will describe to you is a person named Sam. During my time as corporate marketing manager for the pharmacy and optometry division, Sam became president of the drug chain. Within a few days of his arrival at the company, I was sitting in my office working on a project when he knocked at my door. He said,

"Hello, my name is Sam. Do you have a few minutes?" He then sat down with me for about 30 minutes and engage in a low-key discussion. He asked questions about my background, my family, my education and the work that I did. And he told me about himself and his background. We both shared insights on how to improve the company's success, and he seemed interested in my thoughts. When that meeting was over, I felt enthusiastic about the future of our company.

The contrast in the approach between them is stark. One fellow, Dick, believed that he was God's gift to the planet and acted like it. Dick was a complete jerk. Sam was a caring person with a vision for our company's future. Sam came across as competent, professional, and a born leader. Dick came across as a mean-spirited jerk. As an employee of Sam's, I would have come in early, stayed late, and done anything he asked to help our company be successful. As an employee of Dick's, I couldn't wait to find another job and I couldn't wait to see him fail, which he did in spectacular fashion.

And a huge part of the initial reaction to both these individuals was their mindset and the words they used to engage their employees. Dick couldn't help but try to build himself up by making us all look inferior. Sam was a genuine leader who inspired me to excel.

Dick was a dictator. Sam inspired employee engagement. The Jewel Corporation trained Sam. Their leadership style was the "first assistant" philosophy of management. Each manager was to see himself or herself as serving the employees he or she managed.

The store manager acted as the "first assistant" to store employees. He was required to help them solve problems. The manager served the employee's concerns. Jewel considered the store level employees as the "first assistant" to the customers. Employees could make connections, address problems, and use judgement to meet customers' needs. The employees served the customers.

With decades of employee management experience, I believe the Jewel mindset of a manager being the "first assistant" is ideal.

Simpler things are easier to communicate and more likely to be followed. As a first-time manager, you can do fine if you understand employees care about three big things.

1. **They hope to perform important work.** They seek to know the world needs their work. It's important for them to feel like they are doing something useful. It is the good leader's job to remind employees of the important nature of their work.

2. **They seek confirmation of their competence.** No one wants to be known as bad at what they do. Knowing their work is high quality brings pride and confidence. Good leadership is essential for employees to feel confident in their abilities. Effective leaders provide clarity and measure benchmarks to define good work for employees.

3. **Employees want to know that their boss, their organization or their company appreciates the work that they do to help the company be successful.** If I

feel the work is important and I am good at the job, but my company doesn't care about me, I won't be successful. The good leader shows appreciation to every employee. Excellent leaders focus on these three crucial things.

If all three things are available at work, employees will be engaged and productive. If any one thing is missing, then they are just taking your paycheck while they are waiting for something better to come along.

The traditional industrial mindset projects that I am the boss and all my employees work for me. The Jewel mindset projects that I am the "first assistant" who is going to help all of my employees become successful and achieve their career goals. Which do you think will engage your employees?

References

1-State of the Global workforce Report 2023 https://www.gallup.com/workplace/349484/state-of-the-global-workplace.aspx

2- Gallup's Employee engagement survey $Q^{12}$: https://www.gallup.com/workplace/356063/gallup-q12-employee-engagement-survey.aspx

# CHAPTER 2: THE THREE KEYS TO LEADERSHIP

**Engagement is the Key to Success**

Do you know how to get your team to reach its goals? A good leader will constantly assess the mood of the team and analyze the impact of his or her actions. Are your actions helping the team get closer to its goals, or are you preventing the team from reaching its goals?

Managers don't intend to destroy the effectiveness of their team, but they often do. Sometimes frustration, personal biases, or stress can manifest as an emotional outburst. If you get out of line, take ownership and undo the damage. That's part of being a leader.

Bad bosses do not admit they made a mistake. Is what you're doing positive for your team? If it is, do more of it. If it isn't, do less of it, and apologize for your lapse. Before you can hold other people accountable for their actions, you must be able to hold yourself to the standard.

The ability to focus on critical performance issues is essential for your team's success. The textbooks may not agree with this. And you may not find them in your company's policies and procedures manual. They are, however, the true drivers of success.

I was the seasonal buyer for Sav-On Drug company chain back in the 1980s. One of my responsibilities was to organize the Fall trade show. We would bring in all our vendors, all our store managers and assistant managers and layout all the Ad programs for the upcoming season. We showed them the programs we had developed. They could meet with the vendors and see and touch the product. They could place orders for delivery. It was a three-day event at a major convention center, with 500 attendees, 100 vendor booths and a live stage.

My normal work-week comprised 40 hours on a salary basis. Between the hotel, convention center, work, coordinating, problem-solving and meeting with show decorators, I was on the site almost 24 hours a day. I ensured the event's success. Getting the order guides prepared and setting up the electronic order systems took a tremendous amount of time and effort.

By the time we completed the event, I had spent close to 110 hours in the previous seven days at work. The work drained and exhausted me. My family missed me. After three days at the show, I met up with my boss at day's end. I told him, "After a long and taxing week, I'm dead tired. Tomorrow I am going to stay home and sleep all day."

My boss looked at me and said, "You can't do that. Granting your request to skip work tomorrow would be unfair to others."

I could not believe he said that. I just completed this huge event, which was a rousing success, and he was telling me thank you very much, but go to hell.

He snatched defeat from the jaws of victory. He turned a moment of pride and satisfaction into unbelievable, bitter disappointment. I worked extra hard on this project. It was tremendous success by any objective measure. It positively affected every single store in the chain, and then my boss flushed that all away because he couldn't say, "Good job. Take some time and go kick it. You've earned it."

What did he communicate to me as an employee? He conveyed to me that the organization did not value my work.

Mind you, he was not a bad guy. He was a nice person and a gentleman. Despite doing good work, he had a habit of doing a few foolish things each week that undermined it. He was a major impediment to our excellence as a team. He did not understand his role as a manager.

Team success hinges on three issues you must understand if you hope to become a good boss.

**First is Engagement.**

Is the team engaged? Or are they just going through the motions? Are they putting in their hours? Are they just physically present but not engaged in any meaningful work?

Engagement drives the success of an organization. Gallup's Human Sigma project showed that employee engagement leads to customer engagement and higher profits by 30-40%.

Employee engagement and customer engagement are the financial success of any business. You want to encourage engagement, not discourage it. In my trade show story, the boss failed to recognize my hard work for the trade show. And it affected my engagement in the work of our team.

Gallup Research shows that 78% of employees across various professions are not engaged at work. Improving your team is as simple as directing them to the right tasks and inspiring them to engage. Even if only half of your employees taking part, performance would improve. In addition, COVID has brought about Quiet Quitting, where employees do as little as possible at work. Engaging employees in working will be a significant challenge for future managers.

**The second trait to focus on is a concept that I do not know what else to call, so I'm calling it "How to Win Awareness (HTWA)."**

My brother Tom, based on his experience as a baseball coach, explained this to me. Certain players may have a less physical skill, less speed, or less strength. They don't run as fast. They don't throw as hard. And they don't jump as high. They possess crucial skills for winning baseball games under pressure.

This does not get recorded in the game statistics. A batter may roll the ball to the second baseman with a runner on second and no outs to move them to third. From third base a sacrifice fly or a chopper can drive in the runner if there is only one out. The batter gets no credit for this action in the line score because it doesn't count as a hit, but it's a productive out.

Some players know how to position themselves. They understand when to dive, throw, and hit to aid the team in winning.

In business, this happens as well. There are employees who are skilled at smoothing over customer issues and fixing problems. These skills aren't in the policy manual. Some people have a knack for getting the right things done right.

They might not be as fast, smart, or glamorous as other employees. However, they solve problems and advance team goals.

Some individuals excel at advocating for themselves and their objectives. But they don't perform when you need them to. They hinder team success because of their selfishness.

Be careful to distinguish between showmanship and actual productivity.

**The third trait that a leader needs to pay attention to and understand is Role Identification.**

Does each person on your team execute the role assigned to them? Sometimes it's not the role he/she wants, and sometimes it's not the role he would prefer or even in his mind be best at. But does he take on his role and perform his role as the team needs him to do it?

Playing your role well is important for good team chemistry.

A true leader understands the three traits that drive the success of the team:

1. Engagement,

2. How to win awareness, and

3. Role identification and commitment.

Bad bosses cause employees to disengage, reward the wrong people, and allow unproductive behavior to become the norm.

Good leadership requires being a good person. Leaders exhibit the attributes they expect from their employees. And they should not display the negative attributes they don't want in their employees. Good leaders must understand these key drivers of success, but should also be able to assess the impact of their actions on the team. No leader is perfect. We all make counterproductive mistakes. The only way to avoid failure is to not try. Of course, the unintended consequence of trying nothing new is an unproductive team.

Great Bosses can adjust their tone as necessary. The tone of your leadership is your attitude, your demeanor, how loud you are, how engaged you are into the daily activity. Understand that any noise or any sound or any pattern that becomes consistent, recognizable and repetitive gets tuned out.

For example, if you go to bed listening to soft classical music, it fades into the background as you fall asleep. However, if you're sound asleep, and music blares, it's going to jolt you out of your sleep. You're going to wake up and say, "Wait a minute. What was that?"

The leader's tone of voice needs to be adjusted to snap the team to attention when it is required. Good bosses restore the team focus when needed, encourage their success and inspire excellence. A good leader recognizes when the group's energy has waned. Then he or she must provide that impetus to recapture the positive energy needed to succeed. Defining these things is easier than doing them. Good leadership requires putting people in roles that benefit both them and your team. But remember that your role is to nurture the talent available to you to mold a high-performing team of employees.

A quality leader will become a great boss based on their ability to attract, keep, and develop the talent to create a productive team. These three accomplishments lead to the happening:

1. First, foster a climate that unleashes your team's talent. To continue with the baseball analogy, it's not your job to practice hitting, throwing, base running, and pitching. Your task is to create a climate that motivates talent to invest the required time and energy in learning and using those skills.

The key difference between an engaged team and one going through the motions is internal motivation. Engaged teams identify with and buy into the goals and values of the team. They enjoy improving and working hard in order to meet those goals.

2. Second, discover the untapped talents of the person. It is easy when scouting baseball teams for people to recognize the player that can run fast, throw hard, hit for power, hit for average, and be a great base runner. Everybody sees that person. Outstanding players like Willie Mays, Mickey Mantle, Hank Aaron, and Mike Trout did everything well when they were very young.

The best choice for a late round draft picks is more challenging. These players have less apparent talents. Most players will not have obvious, identifiable superstar traits. The typical player doesn't exude power, speed, energy and enthusiasm. When you land a superstar, great, take advantage of it. But until then, you must take what you have and turn them into stars.

3. The third success factor for a leader is fostering an environment for employees to work to their full potential. The culture you create at work will play a magnificent role in your success as a team.

Bad bosses want to get rid of anyone who fails. They threaten employees with termination for every transgression, real and imagined. They create a stressful, miserable and destructive negative mindset environment. Good leaders nurture the work environment to bring out the best in their people. They create safe and enjoyable environments by building patterns of success through praising good work. They offer constructive feedback on how to improve when failure or setbacks happen.

If a teammate is practicing a skill, and gets better at it each time she tries it, her technique is improving. The results of her hard work are visible, which is encouraging. She will be more likely to see that success manifest in performance. Effective leaders build good habits and teach techniques for success to all their employees. The team's success is more likely when their skills are improving. The job requires more than physical talent; you must bring out people's best qualities.

Let's refocus on leadership. Quality leadership is about answering these key questions and making positive changes based on your findings.

- Are you aware of the real performance issues?

- Do they solve problems or do they create them?

- Are you rewarding employees on the right metric?

- Do they know how to win?

- Do your workers feel engaged?

- Is your customer base engaged and recommending your services to others??

- Are you confident that you've put the right people in the right roles to help your team??

- Have you positioned your people to maximize their potential?

- Are you able to adjust the tone as needed to keep your team focused and energetic?

- Do your workers enjoy coming to work and have positive relationships?

- Is their work driven by necessity or passion?

- Can you create a climate that frees talent, identifies abilities, and enables success??

Outstanding leaders can answer these questions affirmatively. Bad bosses wonder why anyone would ask these dumb questions. True leaders create excellent businesses. Bad bosses continue their destructive behavior until the business fails.

# CHAPTER 3: THE THREE CRITICAL MANAGEMENT ROLES

Effective leaders build strong teams. To lead the team towards greatness, you must integrate three roles into your leadership style. Good leaders do these three things well. Bad Bosses do not.

**Coach Role**

The first is Coach Mode. A coach guides each teammate to reach their full potential. Great bosses are excellent coaches, Bad Bosses are not. Effectiveness in coaching requires mastery of three skills. These are:

**1. Vision** - understand what the real end game is. Know what you're trying to accomplish. Have a clear vision of your destination.

**2. Flexibility** - customize directions for each individual teammate. Some teammates require positive reinforcement. Others need a kick in the butt. Some may need a day off. Others may need to work through their struggles. Select individuals need praise. Some need to be left alone. Equal treatment for all does not mean identical treatment for all.

**3. Process** - applying the right technique at the right time to get the best performance. People learn by building patterns of success. They get discouraged when they have patterns of failure. Coaches should incorporate competence and confidence building into their training.

A coach's mission is to develop a teammate to reach their individual potential. Your role as coach is to improve each teammate, so the team becomes stronger and more resilient. (Become a force multiplier)

**Command Role**

The boss must lead when a delayed decision could affect the mission. A competent team doesn't need micro-management, but it requires decisions to be made.

Good bosses will give orders when necessary. But they allow subordinates to struggle when it will aid their development. Bad Bosses micromanage and interfere with good decision-making processes.

Mastering three skills is key to being an effective commander.

**1. Intention** - know the command intent of the mission. Understands the essence of the orders and plan, not just their written or vocalized form.

**2. Recognition** - recognize the game that you're in. Let me use a major league baseball example. In a 162-game season, your team will suffer a significant loss about one-third of the time. You will crush the other team in one-third of the games. They will fiercely contest the final third of the games until the last pitch. Either team can win or lose. Effective leaders learn to recognize the battle situation and make the right decisions that lead to mission success.

**3. Timing** - making the right call at the right time. Players are often unsure of their roles.. The team's involvement in the game/business may hinder them from seeing today's strategy for success. Effective leadership is applying the right burst of leadership when needed. The best bosses make the right call when it counts..

**Create Role**

Effective leaders learn to create an environment in which the team can thrive. Powerful leaders rally the team around the cause by motivating and inspiring them. A great boss motivates the team for present and future success. Inspiring the team to succeed differs from ordering the team to succeed. Great Bosses know how to engage each teammate in creating excellent performance. Bad Bosses create an environment that stifles performance.

I agree with the U.S. Army field manual FM 6-22 statement on leadership. Good Leaders master three skills and inspire others to thrive.

> 1. **Purpose** - keep the team focused on the long-term vision for success.

2. **Direction** - inspire the team to excel by engaging them in the mission.

3. **Motivation** - energizes the process of success.

Leaders teach their teams how to tackle problems and face adversity. Outstanding leaders learn to reward effort and allow their team the freedom to argue their point of view. True leaders inspire their teammates to engage in and believe in the team's mission.

People join wonderful organizations, but they quit bad bosses. The modern employee does not want to be managed, she wants to be inspired. Successful businesses inspire employees with the mission and grant them the freedom to succeed.

Great bosses create an environment where the team can thrive. They push decisions down the organization and give their team the power to decide without fear of punishment.

A Bad Boss paralyzes the team by hoarding decision making power. It shows that only the boss makes important decisions.

Micromanaging all aspects of a complex system is beyond one person's capability in the 21st century. The distribution, customer service, sales, and support teams are likely to have better task knowledge than the executive team does.

For example, in healthcare, the physician makes diagnoses; the pharmacist handles medication; the nurse provides care, and the support staff handles billing. Each of these roles requires a distinct set of competencies. Every business has similar areas of expertise. Involving knowledgeable people improves decision-making.

All stakeholders don't need equal votes to make this input valuable. The executive team still needs to exercise their command role when necessary. But the process for making high-quality decisions requires an open airing of the actual issues.

Far too many teams attempt to avoid conflict at all costs. Teams that avoid arguments don't improve. They never push each other to make mistakes they can learn from. To create the sharpest edge and most durable sword, the blacksmith applies heat and hammer. A good leader balances applying pressure or praise for optimal results.

The internet has altered the competitive landscape. Everyone in the world competes with everyone for everything. Both good news and bad news travel fast. Somewhere in the world wide web, someone is fact checking and criticizing everything that every organization does.

To avoid damaging blows to a company's reputation, your behavior must be above reproach. A mismatch between a company's values and performance will be public for all to criticize. This is unavoidable in the internet age.

And the pressures are even tougher when you are the executive, financial, marketing and sales director for your own firm. You can't master every necessary skill. You need to build a support team that has the complementary skills needed to provide high-quality decisions.

General George S. Patton said this best when he stated,

**"Never tell people how to do things. Tell them what to do, and they will surprise you with their ingenuity."**

He also said, "**Lead me, follow me or get out of my way.**"

General Patton was an unparalleled leader.

# Chapter 4 : The Ten Things You Must Get Right

Let's now focus on steps you can take to help your team. A comparison of what good leaders do versus what bad bosses do, will show some patterns.

Remember:

Your mindset shapes your thoughts, which shape your actions, which become your habits, which form your character, and your character will shape your destiny.

Behaving like a leader is crucial. Even though you may not be a great leader yet, the job is to fake it until you make it. The best way to fake it is to act like you are a great leader. You can achieve success by using these simple concepts below.

## The Top Ten Things You Must Get Right

1. The most crucial thing is to behave in line with your values. Your values need to be centered on positive and upbeat themes such as excellence, empathy, compassion, community, or team. These values should guide your behavior and that of your team. When the going gets tough, you will always fall back on your core values as your key decision-making tool.

2. While it is important that every business makes a profit; it is critical to focus your energy on engagement, not net profits. Maximizing temporary profit gains at the expense of customer engagement can be a fatal error. By creating an army of engaged customers, you can assure the long-term profitability of your business. Building customer engagement is key to profits.

3. High-performing teams have members who believe in their mission and have the freedom to execute their strategy. Only 30% of a work team works towards excellence, with the rest undermining the team's efforts. If you focus your energy on building a strong team dedicated to the right vision, your business will excel.

4. Team members must put team goals above their own interests. A leader's key role in developing a high-performance team is to maintain a focus on team excellence. We should remove teammates that refuse to help the team succeed. Your team is looking for you to

protect them from selfish teammates who undermine their team effort.

5. Engaged customers are essential for successful business. Engaged employees create engaged customers. The real profit drivers in your business are the enthusiasm and energy your team directs towards customers.

6. Decisions get made every day. If a decision is reversible with no serious risk of harm, make it quickly. You can always fix it later with no appreciable harm to the operation. Don't agonize over the decisions that don't matter. Determine a decision's importance by evaluating its impact on the business. If the net impact is minor, then decide and move on.

7. Some decisions are not easily reversible. Examples are purchasing an expensive piece of equipment, signing a long-term lease, or moving into a new building. They require careful analysis of all the potential outcomes before execution.

New managers may not get to make irreversible decisions. But as their career progresses, they will be required to. The ability to balance decisiveness and caution is key for an excellent manager. Make irreversible decisions carefully.

8. The coach's role is critical to a high-performance team. Your goal is to be certain that every employee understands the skills and attitudes you want them to display. Many

new managers do not specify expectations prior to disciplining employees. As a new manager faced with an underperforming employee, I suggest your first step always be to question the person about their training.

Ask them how they received training and what their understanding of the goals of that training was. Proper training can prevent negative encounters between yourself and an employee. I understand that given the time pressures and rapid pace of many jobs, training is difficult. It is unfair to reprimand an employee for lacking training.

Leaders recognize when to lead or when to empower their team. A strong team comprises people who can make accurate decisions without direct supervision. This will never happen overnight. You must let them try to coach them through the process to improve their decision-making skills, otherwise you will never reach this goal. Certain issues are always the manager's responsibility. Bosses should never be delegate critical decisions to another person.

9. Knowing who to hire and who to fire is a key management skill. Despite the stress, you must choose who will join your team. Quick decision-making on these issues helps the team move forward. A perfect case will be when an individual team member has been selfish and unwilling to help the team succeed. Prolonging the decision to fire that employee communicates that selfish behavior has no consequence. Selfish defiant employees need to be removed from the team as soon as possible. This is your job as the manager.

10. Good leaders create the environment for team success. Coaching employees, leading without micromanaging, and shielding your team from bureaucracy, are all important leadership skills.

Every organization has bureaucratic stupidity built into their processes. If this stupidity is keeping your team from getting good work done, it is your job to clear the obstacles for your team. The more you go to bat for your team to get them the resources and freedom they need, the stronger your team will become.

## The Beverly Hills Story Revisited

Let me remind you of the story I began back in the introduction to this book. I encountered several issues on my first day at the new drugstore. Computers were down. I was untrained in the systems and unfamiliar with my colleagues. The individuals assigned to train me failed to appear. The staff was not capable of doing their jobs without supervision. Customers in the waiting area were ready to brawl. I had four clerks and two technicians standing there staring at me, looking for guidance. What you would have done?

Here is what I did.

1. My first thought was to stem the rising anger and frustration of the customers. The lack of information is more intolerable than problems. I stepped up to the waiting area and announced, "Ladies and Gentleman, we are experiencing a catastrophic computer failure. We need time to make the computers operational. Is anyone here to pick up a prescription? Form a line at registers 1 and 2 if you are here to pick up a prescription. If you need to drop off a new prescription, come to register 3. Come to register 4 if you have any other issues. I apologize for the problem, but we will get you taken care of as soon as we can."

2. Getting the system operational was my second thought. I assigned a technician to call tech support and resolve the computer issue.

3. I needed to determine when another pharmacist would

arrive to help me. I checked the schedule and the next pharmacist would not arrive until 11:00 am. I called her to verify she was coming and asked her to come as soon as she could.

4. My next concern was to enforce a process for prescription dispensing. This store filled over 500 prescriptions per day and had no system for alphabetizing their "will call" prescription area. To find a customer's order, the clerk had to sift through 400 filled prescriptions every time. I sent a clerk over to the plastics aisle and had her pull several plastic bins to use in sorting prescriptions. While waiting for the computers to start, I had the team alphabetize and shelve the "will call" prescriptions.

5. As the computers came online, my challenge was to get orders processed. I instructed the staff to sort orders into "Waiting" or "coming in later" stacks. We only worked on orders for people who were waiting until the second pharmacist arrived.

6. I asked every employee to shorten their lunch break from one hour to 30 minutes. I bought pizza and salad for them, so they didn't have to leave the store to eat.

And by the end of the day, we had survived with our sanity intact. Over the next few weeks, we refined our processes and improved our customer service. And because of my leadership, instead of panic, the staff worked together very well. I wouldn't want anyone to have a disastrous start like this. I hope the first day of your new manager's experience is much smoother than what I described.

Here's the key.

You cannot control what life is going to throw at you, but you can control how you react to it. When I have reacted well, I have done well. And when I have not, I have failed miserably. You will mess up sometimes. Do the best you can but always learn from your mistakes.

Leadership is all about how learning to coach, command and create the environment for your team to be successful. And that all begins with a management mindset.

# CHAPTER 5: THE TEN COMMON MISTAKES MANAGERS MAKE

Managers make these ten common mistakes. These mistakes end up costing them respect and hurt the performance of their team. Making these mistakes also causes new managers to get discouraged. Struggling to be successful is very frustrating. These common mistakes will teach you what NOT to do. Good managers should adopt the **Leader Mindset**. People with a **Bad Boss Mindset** do the things listed below.

**1 - Act like a BossHole.** A BossHole (Bad Boss) is a major turkey. A Bad Boss is that person who sucks the life, energy, joy and enthusiasm out of their team. They do this by being disrespectful, selfish, mean, arrogant, and condescending. It takes a certain amount of skill to act like a boss without being overly bossy. People are averse to being told what to do. A boss who is always haranguing employees doesn't understand leadership. We may feign a sense of superiority when feeling unprepared for a new job. Remember, your attitude and mindset will affect everything that you do. Your authenticity is clear to your employees. They can tell if you are sincere. They can tell if you're faking it. Managers don't have to be right. Your job is simply to build a high-performance team. Dick's aggressive approach to entering a meeting and declaring himself the new sheriff was damaging. Sam's approach to calm and competent leadership was much more effective.

If you want to learn how to be a Great Boss, then you should read my previous book, *The BossHole Effect.* This book takes you step-by-step through building a high-performance team.

**2 - Try to Solve Every Problem Alone.** New managers think they have to solve all problems alone. They believe it's their responsibility to provide all the solutions. The problem with this approach is that these thoughts become your actions and habits. Being the sole source of answers will cause people seeking your help for years. It also means that you are teaching your employees not to think for themselves. You are teaching them not to solve their own problems. And you are teaching them they are not as worthy as you are.

I have seen managers interrupting employees during customer encounters. It embarrasses the employee and reinforces your sense of superiority. They will not appreciate this.

Employee feedback may not be workable in certain decision-making circumstances.. I am not suggesting that you abdicate your decision-making authority. You shouldn't relinquish your command decision-making authority. Managers should delegate many daily business decisions to the lowest effective level of the organization. Without delegating, you won't have time for anything else. All decisions go through me is a bad management strategy.

**3 - Say "Because I Said So."** However, that doesn't mean you should exercise that authority. There may be times when you have to decide quickly. But at the earliest opportunity, explain your reasoning and point out why you think it's the best approach. Your team needs to understand the reasons behind your actions in order to understand clearly what your expectations of them are. When you say, "because I said so!" you project, "I am superior." They will interpret this as you think they are inferior. It will appear arrogant and they won't like it.

**4 - Do As I Say, Not As I Do.** Once you assume a leadership role, your employees will constantly watch you for cues about what to do. They will know of your actions and attitude constantly. If you're 10 minutes late, they will notice. Taking a long lunch won't go unnoticed by them. They will know if you denigrate an employee. They will detect your frustration or anger. And they will check you for alignment. If you are telling them to behave a certain way and you are not behaving that way, you will lose their respect. If you make a mistake, call yourself out and inform everyone it's not acceptable. To ensure respect, apply the rules of behavior to all in the organization.

The most important thing you can do as a leader is keep it simple. Craft a simple set of guidelines and then make sure you adhere to them. Here are the ones that I have used forever. They have worked for me. Borrow them if you wish.

Do what's right, treat others well, and strive for excellence.

I incorporated them into my One Page Employee Manual that you can find in Chapter 8.

**5 - Make Dumb Rules.** We ignore rules perceived as stupid. If people ignore one rule, they will lose respect for all rules. Making new stupid rules can decrease respect for necessary rules. I'm a big proponent of as few rules as possible, but strict enforcement of those rules. Be careful about issuing edicts you won't be able to sustain or support in the future.

Inexperienced or poor managers try to create an employee manual that will cover every situation. They want to have signs posted everywhere telling everybody what to do. This will never work. The world always creates a circumstance not covered by your employee manual. Simplicity is key to sustainable and followable rules. Follow-able may not be a word, but it should be. Again see Chapter 8.

**6 - Try To Be Nice to Everyone.** Your employees don't need you to be nice. They need you to be respectful, courteous and consistent. They need you to say what you mean and mean what you say. Trying to be nice can backfire on you. You may start deciding based on how nice it is rather than how right it is. Do what's right, let them decide if they like it.

People do not agree with everything. Trying to be liked is futile. You will gain respect by doing the right thing, at the right time, in the right way. It is much more important that they respect you rather than that they like you. This doesn't mean you should act like a jerk. It just means that you can't let "nice" impede doing what is right. Keeping an employee who can't do their job communicates your standards doesn't count. They will perceive your attempt to be nice as weak.

**7 - Attempt To Treat Everyone The Same.** Treating every employee the same is a serious mistake. No two employees are identical. Policies and procedures are standard, but individuals may have varying interpretations and responses. It is the manager's job to communicate effectively with each employee in order to build a pattern of success in achieving their goals. In order to help each employee succeed, you will need to use different stimuli, different motivation, and different corrections. Different employees may require different methods of encouragement. One employee may need a stern conversation while someone else might need a hug. Your aim is to be the "first assistant" for every employee, not treating them uniformly.

**8 - Try to Impress.** Don't attempt to prove to everyone that you deserve to be a manager. And stop trying to impress everybody with your knowledge. Boasting about oneself is tedious and irritating. Your employees will not appreciate it. If they ask you about what you've done and where you came from, you can talk about it. But there's a difference between answering questions and being out to impress everybody. Again, it comes down to mindset.

You should admit that you do not know everything. There's no shame in not knowing things. However, it is destructive if you pretend to know things you do not know. This will damage your credibility as a manager. It is an acceptable answer to say, "I'm not sure. Let me find out and get back to you."

It is unacceptable to make up an answer. You'll be lucky not to mis-align your team. At worst, you will sow the seeds of destruction for your credibility.

**9- Criticize Errors But Don't Praise Wins.** New managers are vigilant for unacceptable behavior. They keep their eye open for people that are not doing their jobs right. And they miss the biggest opportunity to improve their team because of this myopia. There is nothing more powerful than well-placed recognition of a job well done. Employee of the month contests and other such recognition programs always end up contrived. But employees will always respond positively when their boss says, "that was well done, I appreciate it." If someone does good work, tell them, "This is good work, thank you."

Don't lie if it's not good work. Don't give false praise. But catch your employees doing something good and tell them you appreciate it and you will see a tremendous improvement in their effort.

**10- Act Like Someone Else.** Trying to be somebody else is difficult. Succeeding at being somebody else is impossible. New bosses should consult a mentor for guidance. Existing bosses still fall into this trap as well. Self-Awareness is the key to self improvement. But you need to use your own values to make your own decisions. If you're trying to act like someone else, it will make you look not confident, not capable, or too weak to make your own decisions. Not every decision needs to be original. That would be silly. But the decision should resonate with your own personal values and convictions.

# CHAPTER 6: THE SEVEN NEUROTIC BLOCKS TO LEADERSHIP EFFECTIVENESS

## Turkey Versus Eagle

I will start this section with two contrasting visual images. One is a scrawny, fidgety, goofy looking bird that can barely fly. It is called a Turkey. People keep it in cages and hand-feed it to keep it alive. The other is a powerful, agile bird that can soar for hours. It is called an Eagle. It feeds itself and it is the symbol for courage and independence. Leaders think like Eagles, not turkeys.

Perhaps the best way to help you understand the mentality of a good leader better is to explain the seven neurotic blocks to optimal team performance. In order for your team to perform well, you must eliminate the influence of these seven needs on your thoughts, words, actions, and habits.

**The first neurotic stumbling block to good leadership is the need to be liked.** Leadership is a lonely business. Every time you get promoted up the ladder, you will find yourself with fewer and fewer peers who understand your role in the organization. Understand that a certain measure of loneliness comes with being a manager. Your friends will perceive you in a new light.

Don't get alarmed by it, don't react to it. Don't let it affect the way you behave. Just know that it will happen. You will need to embrace being alone with confidence and self-esteem. You are now the enforcer of the policy and cannot complain about it at the water cooler anymore. Turkeys hang out in gangs. Eagles are perfectly comfortable soaring above the fray.

I did not create this metaphor to insult employees as turkeys. The animal biology world has considerable evidence that a wild turkey is resourceful and engaging. It is the domesticated birds we eat for dinner. Domesticated turkeys do what they are told and don't think for themselves. Not everyone will like you, so don't worry about it. Don't change your behavior just to make friends. If they are worth having as friends, they will accept you as you are.

**The second block is the need for importance.** We all want to feel important. A desire to be needed can lead some to create problems just to save the day. Don't feel that you are "not important" unless someone depends on you. Leaders who are turkeys just wait for a chance to show off their brilliance. They feel empowered when the group needs them to decide a course of action. But the brilliant leader builds a team that can operate effectively in his/her absence.

**Neurotic block three is present in people who always need to be right**. Avoid pursuing a point just to prove you're right. Avoid pursuing a point just to prove you're right. The cost of being right could alienate your colleagues.? Be flexible enough to listen. Be receptive to all ideas. There is no one who is correct or incorrect all the time.. Don't ever discount information solely because of the source. Do not devalue your team by believing you are the only one who can be correct. It's fine to let others be right. Everyone contributes in a collaborative environment on a well-run team.

**The need to be treated fairly is the fourth neurotic block.** Don't feel the need to receive a full hearing on every minor point. Recognize when to fight for an issue and when not to. Don't waste your time trying to prove your point on issues that don't really matter. A person who spends all his time trying to receive his "fair share" is a turkey. And as a manager, you can't get caught up in arguments about fairness. Fairness is in the beholder's eye. If you set standards and high expectations, then the only measurement that matters is effort. Fairness follows a team focused on improvement.

**The fifth neurotic block is the need to procrastinate.** Some people procrastinate because they fear failure, others because they fear success. You should not fear either. Management is an action, while being a person is a state of being. If you fail in a particular management task, you are not a failure as a person. Don't procrastinate. It is the quickest road to failure. Time budgeting improves managerial skills. Making no decision is frequently more disruptive than making the wrong decision.

**The sixth block is the need to value judge.** New managers are prone to judging people as good, bad, or lazy.. Don't value judge people. Judge them based on performance. If you expect a certain behavior, then anyone who performs it well has done it. Anyone who has not performed the behavior well has not done it. Trying to decipher their motives will cause trouble. If you learn to judge performance on strictly behavioral terms, then fairness and fair treatment will take care of itself. Letting one person off the hook while making others adhere to the rules can make your team bicker and undermine cohesiveness. Focusing on behaviorally anchored performance criteria makes disciplining employees far easier to do.

Let me give you an example: When I was the pharmacy manager of a very busy drugstore, I had one pharmacy technician who had a bad habit of always being ten minutes late. (I will call her Suzie) The problem was she was an amazingly productive worker when she got there. She accomplished double in half the time compared to others. I had another technician who was intermittently late and was a below average performer. (I will call her Mary) Suzie was a key part of our high-performing team. And Mary was easily replaceable. Disciplining Mary and giving a free pass to Suzie, could lead to accusations of unfair labor practices. If I had given repeated warnings to Suzie and she failed to arrive on time, it would have forced me to fire a productive employee. But not responding to her behavior could damage team morale.

The key to fairness is treating all behaviors equally. If you value judge an employee as good (Suzie) versus mediocre (Mary), you risk being inconsistent and unfair. Unconscious personal bias may affect your perception of good and mediocre. If that internal bias affects a protected class of worker covered by Federal or State employment law, then you could get in big trouble and pay huge fines.

We all have biases. Some known, some unknown. In order to avoid violating labor laws, create a set of behaviorally anchored performance criteria that are essential to being a member of your team. Applying the same performance criteria to everyone can help you avoid labor law violations. Sometimes people remind you visually of someone from your past that you didn't like. Or their physical appearance doesn't fit your view of what a top employee should look like. What really matters is, can they can do the job? And the only way you know that is to give them a fair opportunity to do it and to judge them by the same performance standards as you judge everyone else.

Here's what happened to the two late technicians. After a private discussion, I discovered Suzie was a night owl. She couldn't get going in time for the 8:30 am early shift. I readjusted the schedule to put her on the middle shift from 10 am–7 pm and she was never late again. I wanted to avoid losing an excellent employee, so I punished her tardiness by making her come in later. Mary continued to be late intermittently. I put her through disciplinary action and she ended up working for someone else.

It is easy to like outstanding employees and difficult to like mediocre ones. Whether you like the person should not influence your management decisions. Make disciplinary decisions based on job performance.

Sidebar Point: It is also easy to dismiss input from a mediocre employee as worthless. But you should be open to hearing all ideas from anyone on your team. Good ideas can come from anyone. Even the weakest employee has value if you have trained them properly. Their capabilities may surprise you when you give them a chance to show you what they can do. Try to find a role that they are good at and helps the team. As a manager, your goal is to maximize employee performance, regardless of their limited skills.

Be honest and clear about the skills and abilities needed for the job and give everyone a chance to show them. Then find a role where each employee can add their own unique value and let them know you appreciate their contribution. Even if their contribution is minor. Otherwise, they will disengage and affect the morale of your team.

I had one employee who worked as a clerk in our pharmacy. She was a sweet lady who was great with customers, but she wanted to become one of our computer input technicians. During some slow times, we let her try out the role frequently. She simply was not fast enough or accurate enough to keep up with the workflow. She could not perform the job well. I had to take her aside and let her know she would not get to be a computer input technician.

The risk with this kind of conversation is that the employee could become demoralized and disengage from the team. How would you handle that conversation? What exactly would you say to her?

Because I had over twenty year's experience as a manager, I could salvage the situation. I would not have been able to have this conversation when I was in my first management job.

Here is what I said. "I know that you want to be an input tech. I assume you want to be one because you think it is a more important job than what you do. But you are the best person I have at keeping the customers in the waiting area relaxed and calm. You are the only one that knows everybody and can keep them happy when we are super busy. You play a huge role in helping us give great customer service. I can't afford to have you not doing what you do best." She remained a key player on our team for years.

**The last neurotic block is the need to resist reality.** The world is full of great ideas and wonderful theories, but that doesn't mean those theories are worth a damn. The world doesn't change just because you believe it should. The world is imperfect, illogical, and full of inconsistencies. You must recognize this and work with genuine issues. Don't waste your time on stuff that doesn't work. Be pragmatic, ask the simple question - does it work?

New managers often think creating a policy statement or hanging a sign solves problems. I have seen this many more times than I can count. A recurrent problem in community practice pharmacy is that customers refuse to do our job for us. When they want to get their medication refilled, they bring the bottle in and ask for more medicine. The pharmacy often needs doctor's authorization for additional refills, causing delays that can take days to resolve. The pharmacist must ensure compliance with prescription dispensing laws while fulfilling customer requests. The silly new manager will fix this problem by posting a sign at the counter that says, "Please phone in your prescription at least three days in advance." and then get angry with customers when they either don't read the sign or cannot follow the guidance.

Expecting normal folks who are living busy lives to manage their prescriptions with that level of detail and attention is a noble cause, and it will never happen. Your time would be better served developing fast and efficient service that can handle the reality that people need their medications when they need them regardless of laws, policies, procedures and signs to the contrary. Believing in change and wanting it doesn't mean it'll happen. Keep your head out of the sand!

Customers don't read signs or follow instructions. They want what they want when they want it. They want to be treated as if there were your best customer. Don't teach your team to follow rigid rules. Teach them to focus on making the customer glad they came to you. A customer who feels special will refer you to their friends and grow your business. A customer who doesn't get treated the way they want to be treated will not care whether your business survives.

**SideBar Note:**

There is a big emphasis placed on customer satisfaction surveys in many businesses. Not only are those surveys annoying, but satisfaction is a low bar. If I rush in to your store to buy something I need and you sell it to me, then I may respond that I was satisfied with the purchase. But if I stop in to your store and your employees make me feel welcome, help me find what I am looking for, and provide amazing service, I may tell all my friends about the experience. Satisfaction is okay. Engaged customers brag about the experience to their friends.

# CHAPTER 7: EAGLE VERSUS TURKEY MINDSET

The difference between good leaders (Eagles) and bad ones (Turkeys) is based on their mindset. Good leaders behave in a way that enhances the effectiveness of their teams. Bad bosses act in a way that is detrimental to their team.

These phrases may seem simplistic. But I assure you these attitudes will help you identify the right behaviors in coworkers and colleagues. Knowing when your people are acting like turkeys helps you correct those behaviors. Recognizing when you are acting like a turkey helps you self-correct.

These behaviors offer insight into existing patterns of thinking. Focusing on them allows you to remain calm and collegial when helping your employees to stop unwanted behaviors. It also allows you to recognize the right behaviors and praise them. Check out the following list of Eagle versus Turkey behaviors.

Eagles know the spirit of the rules,


Turkeys follow rules literally.

**Eagles know when to break the rules,**


**Turkeys never break the rules.**

Eagles know the command intent of directions,


Turkeys only know what they are told.

**Eagles recognize they don't know everything,**

**Turkeys have a tendency to overestimate their expertise.**

Eagles will experiment with new methods,


Turkeys will only do it the way we taught them.

**Eagles recognize and grasp subtlety,**


**Turkeys think everything is black or white.**

**Eagles see the complexity in situations,**


**Turkeys see everything from their viewpoint only.**

**Eagles prioritize the important few from the irrelevant many,**

**Turkeys do things in chronological order.**

Eagles value planning but are flexible enough to change the plans.

Turkeys will not deviate from their rigid plan.

Eagles understand how to create allegiances rather than enemies.


Turkeys degrade and chastise others with impunity.

Eagles have a high self-esteem and their feelings
of self-worth are permanent,


Turkeys have low self-esteem, large egos, and
their self-worth fluctuates with their popularity.

**Eagles operate from the truth.**

**Turkeys operate from assumptions.**

**Eagles can laugh at their mistakes.**


**Turkeys never admit mistakes.**

Eagles build patterns of success in their employees.


Turkeys beat down their employees.

Eagles improve their leadership skills with a growth mindset.

Turkeys are what they are. And they never get better if they keep acting like turkeys.

# CHAPTER 8: THE ONE PAGE EMPLOYEE MANUAL

In Chapters 1 through 7, I have discussed the knowledge, skills, abilities and attitudes required to be a high-quality leader of employees. The rest of this book will focus on forward looking aspirational tools that you can use to become a great boss. Your mindset as a boss must be one where you set the right tone for your team. Your approach to communications must be one in which everyone who works for you feels you are a good listener. This does not mean you have to agree with them, but you should listen and understand what their concerns are. Listening is a lost art form. Your mindset is important and your communication style is critical. But you must also operate from a sound foundation of core values. Your values will form the foundation upon which to build your team.

This Chapter shows an example of a sustainable set of core values. I developed this set over twenty years ago and have used it in several businesses, in my classrooms and in my daily life outside of work.

However, you must develop a set that you own. You can start with my example and rename it. That is fine. If you want to build your own from scratch, that is also fine. But the key is you must make it clear to everyone what your values are and how they need to operate within this value structure.

Since 1975, I have worked in a variety of large businesses. I have been through the onboarding process at least a thousand times as either an employee or an employer with these corporate employers. The process goes something like this. "Here is our employee manual. It covers everything you should and shouldn't do. You must sign and return the last page today."

The person being hired then signs the last page and turns it in, never having read a single page.

What this means is, the company gave you the manual. They were counting on the manual to communicate their policies and procedures. They were counting on the manual to inspire you to become an engaged employee. And you never read the darn thing. You may have convinced yourself that you would read it later. But employees often only refer to the employee manual when facing discipline.

Do you think this is an efficient and helpful way to engage employees and inspire them to work hard in your business?

Well, I don't either. However, I think it is far worse than just inefficient; I think it is actually harmful. Failure to communicate the values you think are important will prevent employees from understanding what is important to you?

Sidebar: Human Resources departments are driven by compliance with labor laws. Therefore, the wording in these manuals is driven by what lawyers tell companies they can and cannot say. The reason you hire lawyers is to either get you out of trouble or keep you out of trouble. So companies defer to their lawyers to keep them safe. The problem is, this is boring, uninspiring and useless for building a high-performance team.

I believe that most people won't read more than one page. Most people need short and sweet instructions rather than long, jargon filled, coma inducing prose. You will be much more effective at building unity around a common set of goals with a 'One Page Employee Manual.'

You may work for a company that forces you to use their manual, but that shouldn't deter you from developing this as an addendum. I tossed the large manual 20-plus years ago and use the one page manual only.

I do this for a variety of reasons.

1. Engaging employees is more effective and takes 10 minutes or less with each new hire.

2. It emphasizes observable behaviors that anyone can describe and recognize.

3. It defends against unemployment claims and wrongful termination lawsuits better than the larger manuals.

4. It allows you to quickly identify and remove mediocre

team members.

Why is it more effective? Because of its brevity, you can go over the entire thing with each new employee. You can make eye contact with them and check for understanding. You can ask questions to make sure they understand. And you can detect misalignment or lack of interest from them. Within a few minutes, you can describe the principles you stand for and what you will tolerate from your people.

Why is focusing on observed behaviors important? Any time you make a verbal correction for an employee, you risk hurt feelings and emotional outbursts. But remember, the actions an employee takes may be right or wrong, but you don't want to imply that they are a bad person because of their actions. If an employee feels you are attacking their character, they will react negatively to your comments. If the employees understand that there is a behavior that needs to be adjusted, they should not feel like there is something wrong with them as a person. You can change your behavior a lot easier than you can change your essence as a person. If they feel they are being reprimanded for something they can't change, then that discussion will not go well. If all they have to do is stop an incorrect behavior, then you increase the chances the conversation will go well.

Why is it better to defend unemployment claims and wrongful termination suits? Because some lawyers are slimy. They will use every trick in the books to find a loophole in your 14 step disciplinary procedure. They will suggest that you didn't follow your policy as described. And then they force you to pay damages.

Why does it allow you to identify and remove mediocre team members? Because if you consistently observe and rate behaviors in real time you will identify those souls that are simply unwilling to follow your rules. As soon as you know they are unwilling then you have the talking points you need to separate them from your company.

Sometimes they are jerks that are just bad employees. And sometimes they just don't have the capacity to do the job. But if you can sit down with them and say, Do you remember when I explained to you the behaviors that I expected from you? Well I just haven't seen those behaviors from you. I think this job is a mismatch for your skillset. I wish you luck in your next job. By focusing on the behavior and not attacking the person , these conversations are much easier to have without being confrontational.

I have been involved in several employment related lawsuits over the years. Employment lawyers are excellent at getting the important evidence kept out of court and suggesting alternative reasons you persecuted their client. They almost always win when they paint the evil company as attacking the poor employee.

I had a case where I fired an employee for stealing. I had captured her on video, taking money out of the cash register and sticking it in her pocket.

My One Page Employee Manual states:

"Honesty-Equipment, supplies, inventory, cash, financial records, customer lists, business reputation, physical plant and customer goodwill are all assets needed for our business to thrive. Squandering, misappropriating, damaging or destroying any of the assets of this organization is unethical."

When I went to the unemployment hearing, I said to the judge. Here is my honesty policy. Here is a video of her putting the money in her pocket. The judge said that looks dishonest to me and denied her unemployment. Since I filed charges and had her arrested, she went to trial for theft. When we got into court, the Jury let her off as not guilty. They let her off because I had received a partial settlement from the insurance company for the theft and they felt she had two kids and didn't need to go to jail. The District Attorney told me the number one predictor of whether a jury convicts a lady is how cute she is. And this young lady was very attractive.

The moral of the story is to do the best you can, but you can never trust the courts to get it right. Give yourself the best chance possible by giving defense lawyers the least stuff to attack.

Engaged employees generate engaged customers, which generates business success.

**Our Core values**

1. Do the right thing even when you don't feel like it and no one is watching.

2. Treat other people as they deserve to be treated even when it is not convenient.

3. Strive for excellence at all times and in all things.

**Business Philosophy and Ethos**

1. Effort-Success is built on the shoulders of failure. People will appreciate your efforts if failure helps you improve. Giving less than your best effort is unethical.

2. Timeliness-Procrastination is the active disregard of your responsibility to perform on time and evidence of a lack of commitment to the task. Failure to meet deadlines is unethical.

3. Responsibility-Be responsible for the consequences of your behavior. The behavior that you model is more important than the words that you speak. Refusing to accept responsibility for the consequences of your actions is unethical.

4. Attitude-Your ability to lift the efforts of others magnifies your value to the organization. It is your job to make everyone else better. Our organization will only thrive if you are successful. Having a poor attitude is unethical.

5. Alignment-It is your obligation to argue passionately and politely for your point of view while a decision is being made. Once the organization decides, it is your obligation to

support that decision with the same passion as if it were your own. Undermining the policy of the organization is unethical.

6. Respect-You don't have to like everyone that you work with, but you need to work together well. Disrespect towards others is unethical.

7. Whining-Whining is complaining without offering a proposed solution. Whining is unethical.

8. Self-Awareness-Self-assessment is the key to self-improvement. Failure to improve is unethical.

9. Honesty-Equipment, supplies, inventory, cash, financial records, customer lists, business reputation, physical plant and customer goodwill are all assets needed for our business to thrive. Squandering, misappropriating, damaging or destroying any of the assets of this organization is unethical.

10. Presence-You must be physically, emotionally, mentally and intellectually present where and when we need you to be. Failure to be present is unethical.

# CHAPTER 9: BEHAVIORALLY ANCHORED SKILLS

Dr. Martin Seligman[1] of the University of Pennsylvania has published extensively about character traits. The literature on this subject has identified a core set of traits that predict whether a person will lead a successful work life. In 2014-2016, I published 2 peer-reviewed journal articles describing a nationwide survey of 38,000 pharmacists. We asked them a variety of questions regarding the attributes they used to decide whether to hire an employee. We compared the 24 character traits below against a set of 24 academic traits, such as good GPA and high test scores. The results were obvious. All 24 character traits rated significantly higher than any of the academic traits. We asked each question in three different ways and each produced the same result. Employers rated the 24 character traits described below as far more important than any academic traits.

After receiving these results, we tested the same traits as a measure of professional behavior with a group of over 150 working preceptors. They unanimously agreed that these traits were a good approximation of the behaviors of a professional person. These traits are not pharmacy specific, as you will see below.

Here are the character traits we used in our research. These are the traits that best correlate to business success. Below the heading for each character trait, you will see a few behaviors that show possession of the trait. These behavioral descriptions make it fairly easy to observe a person and decide whether they possess the trait.

The beauty of using these anchors is that it diffuses the emotion and negative energy associated with someone not behaving as desired. It allows a supervisor and a subordinate to focus on issues such as, "finishing what you started" rather than an employee feeling that their self worth is under attack by being labeled a bad employee. One of the reason so many manager's fail in their duties is because of the uncomfortable nature of needing to take corrective action against an employee. It is too easy to put off that which is uncomfortable and hope that the behavior will change on its own. Unfortunately what actually happens is that the employee continues to repeat the behavior until such time as the boss has reached the limit f his/her tolerance. The pent up anger is then released as emotion and the conversation is confrontational.

But the beauty of observing behaviors and gently correct them as needed is that the emotional outbursts are greatly reduced. Employees begin to understand that your goal is to make them better not fire them and the tension evaporates. I know this sounds too easy but it actually is.

**How to use these skills in hiring to avoid hiring an evil person.**

As I described way back in the introduction, most people want to do good work and if properly motivated they will. I have spent most of this book describing the right and wrong ways for you to behave to get the most of of your people. But before they are your employee you can use your knowledge of character traits to avoid the biggest mistake of all, which is hiring a evil person. Is it harsh to call someone evil. Yes. Should you call people evil? Probably not. But should you allow disengaged, combative, disruptive people to ruin the team spirit of your workplace? No flipping way. These people will destroy your business if you let them. It is your job as the manager or leader to not let them.

What do evil people do that makes them evil? Look at the character traits list on the next page. A good person will rate as at least a 3 and as high as a 5 on each trait. An evil person will rate 2 or below on several traits.

**Good Versus Evil**

A good person will actively participate in work, shows enthusiasm for what they do and invigorates others by their presence. An evil person does the exact opposite. They shirk their duties, whine and complain, and fight with everyone they work with.

A good person will finishes whatever he or she begins, try hard even after experiencing failure, and work independently with focus. An evil person will leave work unfinished, put in very little effort and interrupt others preventing them from working with focus.

A good person will come to work prepared, pay attention and resist distractions, remember and follows directions and get to work right away rather than procrastinating. An evil person will not be prepared, not pay attention, distract others, not follow directions and screw around rather than work.

A good person will remain calm even when criticized or otherwise provoked, allow others to speak without interruption, is polite to all, keeps his/her temper in check. An evil person fusses at people, talks over people, is not polite to anyone, and shouts at others all the time.

A good person gets over frustrations and setbacks quickly and believes that effort will improve his or her future. An evil person is always pissed about something and is never going to change.

A good person recognizes and shows appreciation for others and shows appreciation for his/her opportunities. An evil person only thinks about his or her self and thinks the world owes them a living.

A good person can find solutions during conflicts with others, demonstrates respect for feelings of others, and knows when and how to include others. An evil person picks fights with everyone, doesn't give a damn about anyone else and claims ownership of successes without acknowledging the rest of the team.

A good person is eager to explore new things, asks and answers questions to deepen understanding, and actively listens to others. An evil person doesn't want to learn anything new, does whatever the hell they feel like doing, and doesn't listen to anyone else.

These behavioral anchors, therefore become an essential barometer of whether someone is somebody you want to hire. When you're interviewing a person, just get them talking and asking about situations that have happened in their life. As they're explaining their history listen to how they behave and what they think about the actions of others. It won't be long before you'll see the foot prints in the sand that tell you that a person is simply not somebody you want to take into your team.

A person can not hide their character from you over time but sometimes than can fool you during an interview. Anyone who has hired alot of people in their career has picked some losers. The challenge for busy managers is that frequently when you're looking for somebody it's because you've lost an employee and you're under pressure to fill the slot. When you rush your hiring process, you increase the chance that you might hire the wrong person. But understand that you will make a mistake at some point.

If you do have to hire someone quickly, or you have been unable to smoke someone with poor character out during your interview, you should fall back on Plan B, which is the sheepdog theory of hiring.

**Sheepdog Theory of Hiring**

I learned the sheepdog theory of management from a sheepherder in Ireland. We went on a tour of his sheep farm, where he demonstrated the use of different whistles to have his dogs move the flock up down, left and right on the hill. It was truly amazing to see each dog react to a different whistle, and yet coordinate their efforts to move the flock throughout the pasture. After the demonstration, I asked the sheepherder how long it took him to teach these dogs, these complicated skills. He mentioned that it took about two years to get a dog fully trained. I then asked him if he ever had a dog that was not trainable. And this is when the lightbulb went on for me.

He told me that he can tell within two weeks whether a dog is going to get it or not. If they won't follow directions and are unable to stay focused, they will never have the discipline to be a good shepherd. And looking back on 40+ years of management, I believe the same thing is true when hiring employees. If someone is not focused and lacks enthusiasm in the first two weeks of their employment, they are not magically going to change later. Therefore, when you hire someone use the first two weeks to actively evaluate all the elements of their character to determine whether they are indeed someone that you are willing to invest your time and energy in.

We are all human and will make mistakes. I have hired people just because I liked the way they looked and sounded only to find out they were terrible employees. And I have reluctantly hired someone that didn't look like I thought they should, only to discover later that they were awesome employees. We all have internal biases of which we're not even aware. I remember disliking one person instantly, but simply because they looked like someone I didn't like 20 years ago. But in the world of running a business and managing people, you have to suppress these inner biases and use, a neutral standard of behavior in order to ensure that you are putting the right people on your team and giving them the resources they need to succeed. That is why I heartily recommend the use of these behavioral anchors to become an essential part of your human relations strategy.

I have built an Employee Character Rating Tool based on this research. You can access this free tool here and use it as often as you like. Just scan this QR Code:

# These are the Character Traits Determined to Most Likely lead to Success in Life

## Zest

- Actively takes part

- Shows enthusiasm

- Invigorates others

## Grit

- Finishes whatever he or she begins

- Tries very hard even after experiencing failure

- Works independently with focus

## Self Control–Work

- Comes to work prepared

- Pays attention and resists distractions

- Remembers and follows directions

- Gets to work right away rather than procrastinating

**Self Control - Interpersonal**

- Remains calm even when criticized or otherwise provoked

- Allows others to speak without interruption

- Is polite to instructors and peers

- Keeps his/her temper in check

**Optimism**

- Gets over frustrations and setbacks quickly

- Believes that effort will improve his or her future

**Gratitude**

- Recognizes and shows appreciation for others

- Recognizes and shows appreciation for his/her opportunities

**Social Intelligence**

- Can find solutions during conflicts with others

- Demonstrates respect for feelings of others

- Knows when and how to include others

## Curiosity

- Is eager to explore new things

- Asks and answers questions to deepen understanding

- Actively listens to others

**The 24 Character Strengths-**The complete list of all character traits as described by Seligman. While his research shows these traits are present in adults, not all these traits have been proven to impact success in life. The ones above are the ones for which evidence shows their importance.

1. **Zest:** approaching life with excitement and energy; feeling alive and activated

2. **Grit:** finishing what one starts; completing something despite obstacles; a combination of persistence and resilience.

3. **Self-control:** regulating what one feels and does; being self-disciplined.

4. **Social intelligence:** being aware of motives and feelings of other people and oneself.

5. **Gratitude:** being aware of and thankful for the good things that happen.

6. **Love:** valuing close relationships with others; being close to people.

7. **Hope:** expecting the best in the future and working to achieve it.

8. **Humor:** liking to laugh and tease; bringing smiles to other people; seeing a light side.

9. **Creativity:** coming up with new and productive ways to think about and do things.

10. **Curiosity:** taking an interest in experience for its own sake; finding things fascinating.

11. **Open-mindedness:** examining things from all sides and not jumping to conclusions.

12. **Love of learning: mastering new skills or topics on one's own**

13. **Wisdom:** being able to provide good advice to others

14. **Bravery:** not running from threat, challenge, or pain; speaking up.

15. **Integrity:** speaking the truth and presenting oneself sincerely and genuinely

16. **Kindness:** doing favors and good deeds for others helping them; taking care of them.

17. **Citizenship:** working well as a member of a group or team; being loyal to the group.

18. **Fairness:** treating all people the same; giving everyone a fair chance.

19. **Leadership:** encouraging a group of which one is a valued member to accomplish

20. **Forgiveness: forgiving those who have done wrong, accepting people's shortcomings**

21. **Modesty:** letting one's victories speak for themselves, *not* seeking the spotlights

22. **Prudence/Discretion: being careful about one's choices, not taking undue risks**

23. **Appreciation of beauty:** noticing and appreciating all kinds of beauty and excellence

24. **Spirituality:** having beliefs about the higher purpose and meaning of the universe

1 Peterson, C. and Seligman, M. E. P. (2004). *Character strengths and virtues*. Oxford: Oxford UP.

# LEADERSHIP RAPTOR BOSS RATING TOOL

As a reader of my book you now have lifetime access to my Boss Self-Rating Tool to gauge your progress in becoming a good boss and leader. Scan the QR code below to get access.

**Click on the Start The Survey Button**

Accurate self-assessment is the key to self-improvement. If you are not honest with your evaluation of your current status you will not be able to identify the things you need to do to improve. Unfortunately, most people are conditioned by 12-16 years of our academic system to try to get the right answer rather than truthfully identify your weaknesses. This is a huge problem. And it is one you can fix right now by being brutally honest with yourself.

**Complete the survey honestly and obtain your score.**

No one is perfect. The best of us are sometimes performing less than our best. If you rate yourself as perfect, you are likely exaggerating your actual performance. This score gives you a snapshot of how you performed over the last year of activity.

**Identify your weaknesses and educate yourself to improve.**

Taking a survey will not make you a better leader. But using the survey to identify weaknesses and develop a plan to get better certainly will. There is no one right personality for a leader. A good leader is one who performs his/her leadership skills to the benefit of his/her team or business. Good leaders get good stuff done. Bad leaders keep their team from getting good stuff done.

# CHAPTER 10: THE TEN COMMANDMENTS OF GOOD LEADERS

When Moses came down from Mount Sinai he carried a set of stone tablets with a solid set of foundational rules to live by for all of us. I do not claim to be Moses or anything close to a holy man. But I do believe that having a set of Ten Commandments for your management role is a good thing.

1. VALUES ARE MORE IMPORTANT THAN PROFIT.

2. PROFIT IS A BY-PRODUCT OF EXCELLENCE.

3. STRONG TEAMS EXCEL.

4. TEAM INTEREST OVER SELF-INTEREST.

5. ENGAGED CUSTOMERS ARE THE BY-PRODUCT OF ENGAGED EMPLOYEES

6. MAKE REVERSIBLE DECISIONS QUICKLY.

7. MAKE IRREVERSIBLE DECISIONS SLOWLY.

8. COACH TO BUILD PATTERNS OF SUCCESS.

9. COMMAND ONLY WHEN NECESSARY.

10. CREATE THE ENVIRONMENT FOR EXCELLENCE.

As I said, at the beginning of this book, this is a primer on how to be a good boss. It is not a complete textbook on how to be a good boss. The problem with writing some massive tome to cover everything you need to know in order to be a good boss, is that nobody would read it. Therefore, I know that if you have read this book, you will have more questions than answers. The challenge becomes. How do you take the next step to become a great boss and a great leader?

There are all kinds of authors and gurus, offering and selling programs about how to be a good leader. Some of them charge thousands of dollars to hear what they have to say. If you have thousands of dollars to spend on leader ship training, then consider one of those options.

However, if you are on a limited budget, but still need guidance and help on your journey towards becoming a good leader, you may want to consider going to my website at **leadershipraptor.com.**

As part of this journey, I will do my best to help you get the skills you need to thrive as a manager, as a business owner, and as a leader. For some reason in America, we have this strange notion that what we do at work is different than what we do at home and it's different than what we do in our spare time. Leadership is not some thing you leave at the door when you head home from work.

I have used these leadership skills as a businessman, as a boss, as an educator, as a parent, as a coach, as a friend, and as a spouse. Character matters. Leadership matters. Our world is sadly devoid of people willing to take a stand and run their businesses and their lives the right way. And too many businesses lately have decided that they need to voice their political agendas.

Leadership has nothing to do with politics. Good leadership must create value for other people. The only way you can create value for others is to act in a way that puts their needs ahead of your own. As a longtime business owner, I learned the hard way that the world does not owe me a living. When I have been successful it is because I have discovered something that people wanted or needed and found a way to give it to them. When I have had successful operations it's been because I've hired the right people and let them do their jobs. When we focus 100% of our efforts on serving others money and profits seem to fins us. It is karma.

Please check out my website to find more resources as you learn to become an exceptional leader. www.leadershiptaptor.com

If there is anything I can do to help you on your journey, please get in touch you can find me at leadershipraptor.com. I wish you all the best.

# EARN A FREE GIFT

Hey there, fellow leaders and aspiring bosses!

Have you ever wondered how you can make a difference in someone else's life? How you can contribute to the growth and success of others, while experiencing greater fulfillment yourself? Can you review the book "Leadership Skills for Managers Simplified: Master the basics of being a good boss?"?

Now, you might be wondering how a review can possibly deliver value to others during your own reading or listening experience. Let me explain. When you leave an honest review, you provide valuable insights and feedback to potential readers who are considering whether this book is right for them. Your words have the power to guide others towards a resource that can help them develop essential leadership skills and become effective managers. Your review can be the deciding factor that helps someone take their leadership journey to new heights!

So, why do we need your review? Well, it's simple. The world needs good bosses. The workplace can be a challenging environment, and skilled leaders play a crucial role in creating a positive and productive atmosphere. By sharing your thoughts about "Leadership Skills for Managers Simplified," you're helping us reach more people, spread the knowledge, and empower others to become exceptional leaders. Your review has the potential to inspire and guide countless individuals on their path to becoming the best bosses they can be.

So, here's my humble ask: Could you take a few minutes out of your day to leave an honest review? It's super easy! Just head over to your favorite online bookstore or platform, such as Amazon, Goodreads, or even your blog, and share your thoughts. Tell others about the practical tips, the engaging writing style, and how this book has positively impacted your perspective on leadership.

Your review matters. It's not just a few sentences on a webpage; it's an opportunity to make a difference. By leaving a review, you become a part of a supportive community of leaders and entrepreneurs who understand the importance of sharing knowledge and helping others succeed.

Oh, and did I mention the positive impact it can have on you too? Leaving a review not only introduces something valuable to someone else's life, but it also showcases your generosity and goodwill. Other entrepreneurs and leaders will appreciate your contribution, and you never know how this simple act of kindness might come back to you in unexpected ways.

So, my friends, let's spread the word about "Leadership Skills for Managers Simplified" and create a ripple effect of exceptional leadership. Leave your review today and be a catalyst for positive change!

## BONUS GIFT

Authors live and die by the quality of their reviews on Amazon. I have worked extremely hard to put a quality book with helpful advice in your hands. If you have enjoyed this book and have some good things to say about it, please leave a review on my Amazon review page using the account you used to buy the book. Amazon gives much higher credence to book reviews they know are from real people who have actually purchased the book. They also discourage reviews from friends and family. In this way,it provides the best experience for Amazon shoppers. Unfortunately, in the internet world of anonymity, people with snarky things to say write more reviews than people with nice things to say. If you have a positive comment to make please take a few minutes to leave a verified review.

Once you complete your review, take a quick picture of your review and email it to me at: Greg@LeaderShipRaptor.com. I will send you access to a special E-Course Video Series *How to Use The Amazing One Page Employee Manual to Improve Your Business.* *(65 minutes. of content)*

Thank you for your time, your insights, and your dedication to becoming the best boss you can be.

Here is the steps to leave a review:

1. Visit your account on Amazon and Goodreads. Use the Amazon account you used to purchase the book even if it was a free promotion for the Kindle download.

2. Find the book "Leadership Skills for Managers Simplified."

3. Click on the "Write a Review" or "Leave a Review" button.

4. Share your thoughts, insights, and experiences honestly.

5. Click "Submit" and pat yourself on the back for making a difference!

Remember, your review is more powerful than you think. Together, let's transform the world of leadership, one review at a time!

With gratitude,


**Greg L. Alston**

# ABOUT THE AUTHORS

**Greg L. Alston**

Greg L. Alston is the owner of RXVIP Concierge. His company provides Comprehensive Medication Management solutions to Doctors and patients. From 2007-2020, he was a Professor of Pharmacy Management and dean at two different schools of pharmacy. He has a unique resume of management success. He graduated cum laude with a Doctor of Pharmacy degree from the University of the Pacific while simultaneously becoming a credentialed K-12 teacher through the School of Education. During his years in the chain drug industry, he was the first in his graduating class promoted to pharmacy manager, and was the first pharmacist to become corporate training manager, marketing manager and general category manager on the buying staff for Sav-On Drugs. He became a Regional Pharmacy Manager for Thrifty Drugs, and the California Regional Pharmacy Manager for Smith's Food and Drug. After 15 years in the chain drug industry he founded and operated Dracula's Castle Halloween shops and Best Pharmacy and Medical Supply in Southern California.

During his business career he has supervised thousands of employees, worked for hundreds of bosses, and battled organizational stupidity at every turn. After selling the healthcare businesses in 2007 he "retired" to become the Assistant Dean for Assessment at Wingate University School of Pharmacy and within 18 months earned the National Award for Excellence in Assessment from the American Association of Colleges of Pharmacy in 2009. As the Campus Dean for South University School of Pharmacy, he taught Pharmacy Management, Community Health Outreach and Pharmacy Communications Skills courses. As the chief operations officer for the School he was responsible for Human relations, training, revenue and budgeting for all faculty and staff. He frequently consults with corporate clients looking to solve their most perplexing problems.

He began coaching Girls Fast-pitch softball when his daughter Valerie began playing in 1991. Teams he coached reached the national tournament finals for their age bracket, nine times in 10 years with eight top ten finishes, including two national championships. Dr. Alston draws on his experience as a teacher, pharmacist, leader, boss, coach, parent, iconoclast and occasional BossHole to demystify becoming a Great Boss. He and his high school sweetheart, June, have been married since 1976, and jointly raised two children, seven dogs, and innumerable employees. He has an uncanny ability to communicate complex subject matter in clear, simple terms and has been known to not only call a spade a spade, but to sometimes refer to it as a F**KING shovel.

Greg's greatest gift is the ability to turn complex subjects in to clear and simple instructions. His favorite quote is from Albert Einstein:

**Everything should be made as simple as possible, but not simpler.**

## Valerie R. Alston

Valerie R. Alston is the type of daughter that everyone would be proud to have. She was an excellent student, earning high school valedictorian and numerous other honors. She was a gifted athlete earning national titles, state championships, a major college athletic scholarship and several other individual awards. But more importantly, she is a calm, competent competitor, a loyal teammate, a natural empath, an enthusiastic teacher, an unconditional friend, an intuitive leader and only an occasional Daughter Hole. After spending 48 weekends per year playing, talking and living fast-pitch softball with Coach Greg, she has taught him everything he knows about how to be good at what he does. Her wisdom, experience, and guidance permeate every page of this book.

Valerie Alston has been a Master Resilience Trainer-Performance Expert with the Army's Comprehensive Soldier and Family Fitness Program since 2008. She earned her B.S. in kinesiology while playing college softball for the University of Minnesota. After 15 years of playing and competing in softball at the National Level, she fell in love with the mental and emotional side of performance and earned a Master's Degree in Sport Psychology from Boston University. Building on her experiences as an elite athlete and her education in sports psychology, she earned recognition as Certified Mental Performance Consultant (CMPC®) with the Association of Applied Sport Psychology. She has traveled the world from Germany, to Kuwait and Korea, training Soldiers and their families how to use mental skills, to be at their best, when it matters the most.. Valerie draws on her experience as an athlete, exposure to good and bad leaders, her training in Sport Psychology and her work with the military to define good leadership and drive optimal performance. In addition to her work with the Army, she owns Valston Coaching LLC and has developed the Mental Edge Maximizer course and the Toughness trainer app. You can download the app for free from the Google Play or Apple App Stores. Or go to her website at www.valstoncoaching.com She is also the Best Selling author of the Book: Confident Calm and Clutch: How to Build Confidence and Mental Toughness for Athletes Using Sports Psychology. Available on Amazon.com.

# OTHER BOOKS BY GREG L. ALSTON

The Bosshole Effect: Three Simple Steps Anyone Can Follow to Become a Great Boss and Lead a Successful Team. Alchemy Publishing Group Copyright 2014 Available on Amazon.com

The Bosshole Effect: Three Simple Steps Anyone Can Follow to Become a Great Boss and Lead a Successful Team

Own Your Value; The Real Future of Pharmacy Practice Alchemy Publishing Group Copyright 2019 Available on Amazon.com

The Ten Things a New Manager Must Get Right From the Start Alchemy Publishing Group Copyright 2014. Out of Print This book is a updated version of that book.

Made in the USA
Las Vegas, NV
23 April 2024

89042978R00075